The HUMMINGBIRD
OF
El CONQUISTADOR

Elaine A. Powers

Illustrated by Nicholas Thorpe

Dedication
This book is dedicated to the staff of
the El Conquistador Gift Shop and
the hummingbird who shared her life with them.

The Hummingbird of El Conquistador

By Elaine A. Powers

ISBN: 9798849859064 (paperback)

Published by Lyric Power Publishing LLC, Tucson, Ariz.
Design and production by Wynne Brown LLC.

THE HUMMINGBIRD OF EL CONQUISTADOR

ELAINE A. POWERS

ILLUSTRATIONS BY NICHOLAS THORPE

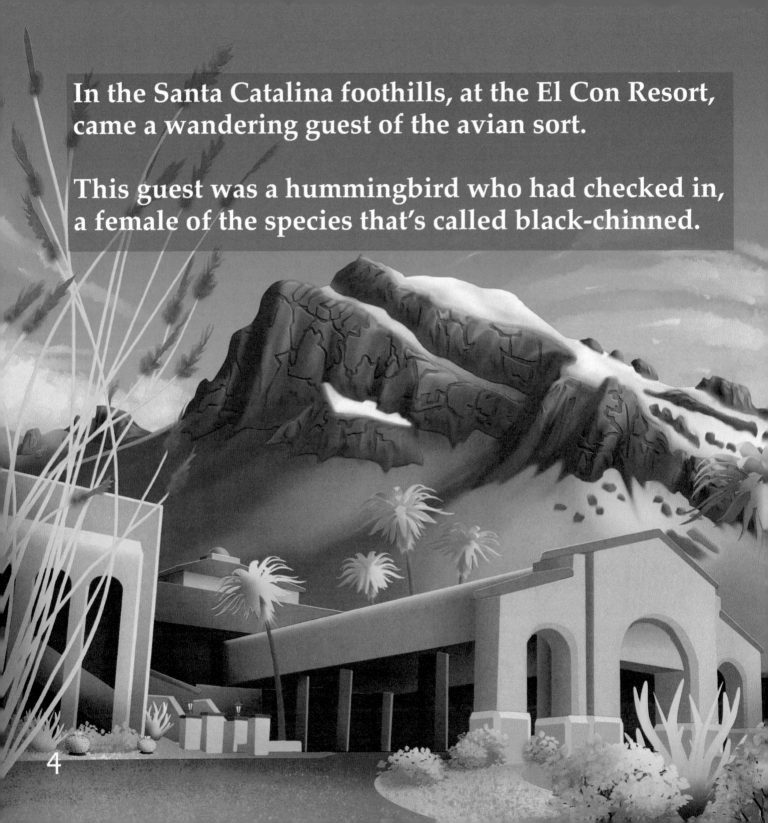

In the Santa Catalina foothills, at the El Con Resort, came a wandering guest of the avian sort.

This guest was a hummingbird who had checked in, a female of the species that's called black-chinned.

Outside El Con's gift shop window,
   the branch was bare,
      until one fine day when the small bird alighted there.

She'd arrived in the Sonoran Desert in Spring,
   flying with eighty times per second undulating wings.

5

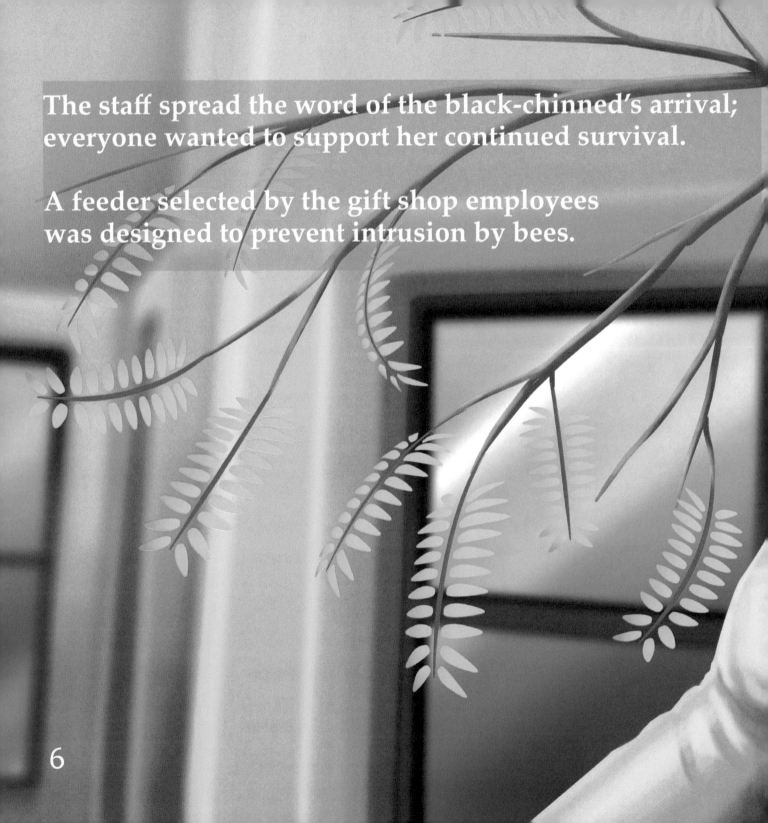

The staff spread the word of the black-chinned's arrival;
everyone wanted to support her continued survival.

A feeder selected by the gift shop employees
was designed to prevent intrusion by bees.

They placed it near their window,
up in a tree –
the perfect location
for people to see.

Black-chinned hummingbirds prefer areas with trees,
Along rivers and canyons, which have a nice breeze.

Black-chinned hummers eat diverse types of food,
including a drink of nectar, when she's in the mood.

Every fifteen minutes, she'd hover and sip,
since flowers only make nectar in a miniscule drip.

8

Flower to flower, among the thousands, she'd speed
and eat small insects for the protein she'd need.
She'd catch insects in flight, on plants, or on the ground,
eating one or several in succession,
consuming any she found.

That high barren branch was her favorite perch.
When she needed to nest, she knew just where to search.

Of course, before she started to build her nest,
a male became her mate after swooping his best.
He made his wings whir in a pendulum dance,
to put the female in the mood for romance.

The sun glinted off his back's metallic green,
and his throat, how it flashed with a purplish sheen.

His efforts paid off and resulted in mating.
Then off the male sped – other females were waiting!

The female chose to build near the gift shop entrance, placing her nest on a horizontal, dry branch.

Why did the hummingbird build her nest there? Couldn't she have built it most anywhere?

The exposed nest site made the staff worry so - such a flimsy, bare branch outside of their window.

"Will the hummer be happy near our resort's main door, with all the guests' comings and goings galore?"

12

13

They watched as she built a compact, deep cup,
then laid two white eggs that filled the nest up.

A couple of weeks later, the naked chicks emerged.
"Feed us more food!" their mother was urged.

14

The chicks grew larger –
the nest expanded, though,

as it stretched to accommodate the thriving duo.

15

A monsoon arrived one day,
                      whipping the branch around.
"Oh no, are the chicks in danger of
                         being flung to the ground?"

The branch flipped,
        spun,
                bent far to the side,
and whipped around,
           flinging the nest with the birds inside.

17

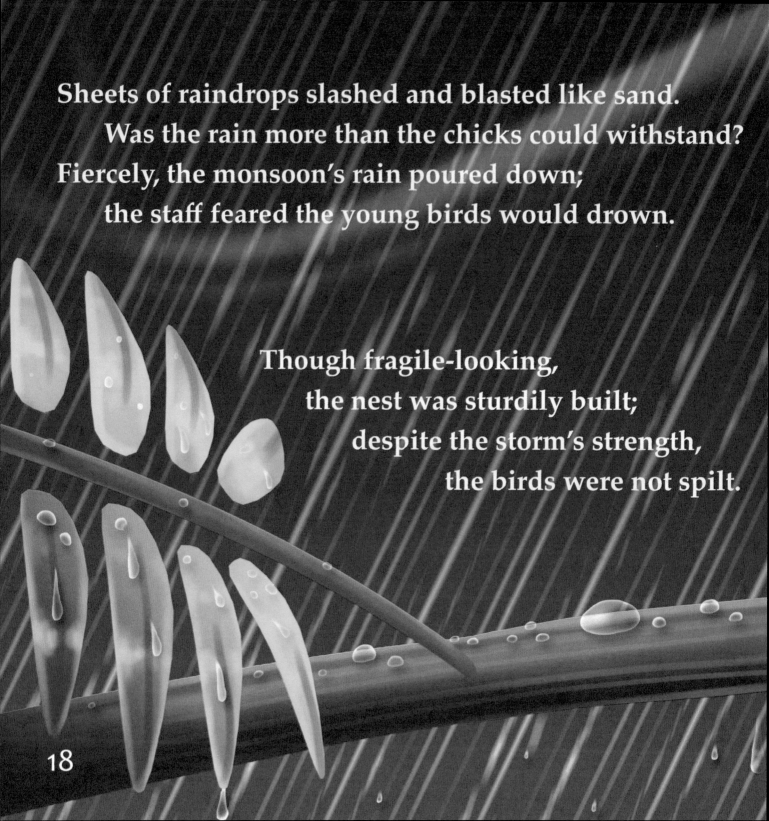

Sheets of raindrops slashed and blasted like sand.
Was the rain more than the chicks could withstand?
Fiercely, the monsoon's rain poured down;
the staff feared the young birds would drown.

Though fragile-looking,
the nest was sturdily built;
despite the storm's strength,
the birds were not spilt.

18

Yes, they both survived and were able to fledge;
seeing them fly off was the staff's great privilege.

20

With cold weather coming,
   off the black-chinneds did go,
   to spend the winter
      in warmer Mexico.

21

Next spring, the mother returned
to where her nest had been,
but the gardener had decided
her branch needed a trim.
With the loss of her favorite resting tree,

22

what would her reaction to this problem be?

Around she flew, quite intent on her search
to locate a suitable replacement perch.

She decided
a neighboring tree branch would do,
and happily, her perch and nest
would still be in view.

If you visit El Con
and hope this special bird you'll see,
outside the gift shop window
is where she might be.

Black-chinned Hummingbird, *Archilochus alexandri*

The black-chinned hummingbird isn't the most famous hummer of the Sonoran Desert – that title belongs to the Anna's, *Calypte anna*. However, the black-chinned is often seen around the area. These small (about 3 inches) hummers live in a variety of habitats: mountains, woodlands, and chaparral. They tend to breed in open semi-arid environs. They live in the western US, northern Mexico, and southern British Columbia. They spend their winters in Mexico, migrating north for breeding season.

Black-chinneds feed on nectar with their long extendable tongues, assisting in pollination. They also eat insects, catching them while flying, or plucking them from plants or from the ground.

The adult males are vividly colored metallic green on their backs and flanks, ending in a dark forked tail. They have black faces and chins, the reason for their common name. Glossy purple throat bands add a final flourish. The females are less colorful and lack the throat patch. These birds have at least five different vocal chips.

During courtship, the black-chinned male flies in a "pendulum" display, creating whirring sounds as he flies back and forth in an arc.

The female builds a nest on an exposed horizontal tree branch about four to twelve feet above the ground. The nest is constructed of grasses, plant fibers, and spider webs. The outside of the nest is covered with dead leaves and other debris for camouflage. The nest can stretch and expand as the chicks grow. They are eaten by bird- and insect-eating animals.

It's been suggested that a nest site close to nests of larger, predatory birds is desired for protection. These predatory birds don't bother with prey as small as hummingbirds. Perhaps the hummingbird in this story felt the human traffic at the resort provided protection for her nest.

Two eggs are laid per nest and are incubated for about two weeks. The chicks hatch featherless and with their eyes closed. It takes about three weeks for them to grow a complete set of feathers. At that time, the chicks can fledge.

The History of the El Conquistador

If our black-chinned hummingbird had arrived at the El Conquistador in 1928, she would not have found it in its present location, the foothills of the Santa Catalina Mountains on the north side of Tucson. The original El Conquistador hotel was constructed on 120 acres on Broadway Boulevard.

The hotel, designed in the Spanish Colonial Revival style by architect Annie Graham Rockfellow (1866-1954), was extraordinary. Even today, the inclusion of tennis courts, riding stable, and barber shop, along with a pool and cocktail lounge, would make the hotel unusual. Unfortunately, the hotel was not financially successful and was demolished in 1960; it was replaced with the El Con Shopping Center. However, the iconic bell tower with its copper dome is preserved at the Casa Blanca Plaza.

In 1982, the hotel was reopened in Oro Valley as the Sheraton El Conquistador Resort & Country Club. The current hotel is located at the base of Pusch Ridge in the Santa Catalina Mountains. The land was once part of the Cañada del Oro Ranch owned by George and Mathilda Pusch. Stagecoaches often stopped at the ranch in the 1870s, so it's fitting that modern travelers also enjoy this scenic area of the Sonoran Desert.

The resort became the Hilton Tucson El Conquistador in 2002. Local owners purchased the property in 2014 and renovated the resort in 2017.

The history of the El Conquistador was provided by the Oro Valley Historical Society, the *Arizona Daily Star*, and Dirk Arnold of Endangered Architecture. You'll find this history posted on a wall outside the resort gift shop, which is located off the lobby.

Of course, if you look in the trees outside, you just might see a hummingbird.

Acknowledgements

One of the joys of being in the book business is the terrific people you meet. The manager of the El Conquistador Resort gift shop, Laura Shook, was kind enough to include several of my titles in her book selections. Subsequently, Laura asked me to write about the hummingbird who had built her nest outside her office window. This book is the result of that inspiration.

I'm often asked if I am also the illustrator, but I am very fortunate to have artists far more capable than I am. These creative and colorful illustrations were created by Tucsonan artist Nicholas Thorpe. He was able to bring a realistic touch to the resort as well as the hummingbird.

I greatly appreciate the assistance of my critique group members, Lori Bonati, Susan M. Oyler, Brad Peterson, and Kate J. Steele. I couldn't do it without them. I also couldn't create this book without my editor and designer, Wynne Brown.

I hope the information included about black-chinned hummingbirds and the El Conquistador resort is accurate. If not, the mistakes are entirely my own.

Elaine A. Powers, originally from Peoria, IL, currently resides in Tucson, Arizona. After a career as a laboratory biologist, she is now pursuing her dream of writing science-based children's books and murder mysteries as well as continuing her work as a citizen scientist for iguana conservation. Her iguanas and tortoises continually inspire her.
For more information, visit her website www.elaineapowers.com as well as the publisher's webpage www.lyricpower.net.

A nearly native Arizonan, Nick Thorpe graduated from the Savannah College of Art & Design (SCAD) in Animation. He uses his talents in visual arts working with marketing and merchandising firms and a freelance practice.
An avid outdoorsman, he loves country with trees, cloudy days, and wide-open spaces.
Visit his website www.nickthorpe.xyz

More books by Elaine

Don't Call Me Turtle!

Don't Make Me Fly!

Don't Make Me Rattle!

Queen of the Night: the Night-blooming Cereus

How Not to Photograph a Hummingbird

Curtis Curly-tail and the Ship of Sneakers

Curtis Curly-tail hears a Hutia

Curtis Curly-tail is Lizardnapped

Curtis Curly-tail is Blown Away

Grow Home, Little Seeds

Bahamian Boas: A Tabby Tale

Tabby and Cleo: Unexpected Friends

The Dragon of Nani Cave

The Lime Lizard Lads and the Ship of Sneakers

Silent Rocks

Fly Back to the Brac, Brian Brown Booby

Clarissa Catfish Visits the Peoria Riverfront Museum

Clarissa Catfish at the Peoria PlayHouse Children's Museum

Guam: Return of the Songs

And several iguana identification booklets, anthologies, and audio theatre scripts